1,001 Advertising Cuts from the Twenties and Thirties

Compiled and Arranged by

Leslie Cabarga, Richard Greene
and Marina Cruz

DOVER PUBLICATIONS, INC.
NEW YORK

1,001 Advertising Cuts from the Twenties and Thirties is a new work, first published by Dover Publications, Inc., in 1987.

DOVER *Pictorial Archive* SERIES

Manufactured in the United States of America
Dover Publications, Inc., 31 East 2nd Street, Mineola, N.Y. 11501

Library of Congress Cataloging-in-Publication Data

1,001 advertising cuts from the twenties and thirties.

(Dover pictorial archive series)
    1. Advertising—United States—History—20th century—Pictorial works. 2. Wood-engraving—20th century—United States.
I. Cabarga, Leslie. II. Greene, Richard, 1953- . III. Cruz, Marina. IV. Title: One thousand one advertising cuts from the twenties and thirties. V. Series.
HF5813.U6A525   1987   659.13′2′0973   87-15546
ISBN 0-486-25490-9 (pbk.)

Introduction

This book is an appreciation of the black-and-white spot illustrations and printing cuts that fill a special place in the history of advertising and printing. In the 1940s, designers such as Lester Beall and Paul Rand became enamored of the "quaint old" wood engravings of the turn of the century. They helped make it "smart" to incorporate them into otherwise modern ad designs. These cuts have had wide use, which continues with the publication of many compilations gleaned from old *Harper's* and other magazines and the many type catalogues that usually contain sections of random cuts applicable to a wide variety of printing needs. The term "cut" refers to the woodcut and, later, to the action of the acid which cut into the surface of a metal engraving. These metal engravings were then mounted on small cuts of wood with small brads. Together they were "composed" with metal type to make up a complete printing plate.

We feel it is necessary to present, finally, a collection of the second generation of small stock advertising cuts—those from the 1920s through the 1940s. The material in this book was culled from old magazines, newspapers and books and from many catalogues issued by firms that sold cuts to printers. These illustrations were then shown to printing customers who used them to enhance a business card, menu or other advertising medium. Since stock cuts seem to have been shared by various companies, a series of images obviously drawn in the 1920s might appear in a catalogue as late as the 1960s.

One catalogue from the mid-1930s was entitled *Type Peps.* The terrific illustrations it contained were used merely to pep up type! Consider some of this stock art: the quality of the line drawings, the masterful use of light and shadow, the sensitivity to reproduction and overall good design. Yet that book might have been titled *Forty Years of Hack Art,* for few of the artists represented in it are known today, though their work is often of excellent quality. Hundreds of artists on staff at newspapers and at agency bull pens, unknown even in their era, labored day after day to satisfy the never-ending need for small-space advertising art. Much of their work was of a high caliber because of the contemporary emphasis on draftsmanship and formal art training. In today's market the successful illustrator is frequently one with the clever idea, not necessarily one with the ability to draw a human figure adequately.

Considering the amount of work that must have gone into any one of these illustrations, this book has been years in the making (in drawing time alone). Each spot is a complete work of art in miniature, requiring no less effort than the larger-scale illustration. The toughest aspects of working any piece of art are usually the concept, design and basic drawing. Although the size of these cuts is small, the original art was frequently done as much as 600 percent up. In fact, the art instruction books of the day recommended the practice as it was felt the best reproduction could be obtained in this manner. It was essential then that the artist plan his line weight to withstand reduction and reproduction. The letterpress printing of the old newspapers and magazines often did not reproduce as true an image as does today's offset printing. (But letterpress printing was blacker.)

The small spot illustration should incorporate the same qualities that make up a good poster: It must at once compel, inform, attract and provide a single simple message. It must be designed with the intended size of reproduction held clearly in mind. Thus the criteria for selection of every illustration in this book were that each form a complete image in itself, have its own innate balance and possess a nostalgic appeal. There is something specifically of an old style about these spots. I once commented to an artist friend that it was very difficult to capture the quality of line or design or whatever it was that gave twenties and thirties ad art its distinctive look. He replied, "Why bother?" Well, to those of us who love such art this book is dedicated.

LESLIE CABARGA

HAPPY NEW YEAR

OLD FASHIONED

MANHATTAN

SIDE CAR

DINE & DANCE

HAPPY·NEW·YEAR

I Resolve

New Year Resolutions

Be my PRETTY VALEN-TINE

LOVE LETTER BOX

TO MY VALENTINE

Sweets for the Sweet-heart

TO MY VALENTINE

SPECIAL for HUSBANDS
Don't Forget!

Fine Candies

FEB. 14th

Candy

Easter

Easter

GET MARRIED BOYS

THANKSGIVING

THANKSGIVING

Thanksgiving

Thanksgiving

SWEET CIDER

Merry Christmas

SEASON'S GREETINGS

Merry Christmas

MERRY CHRISTMAS

THE SEASON'S GREETINGS

GREETINGS

Christmas

Merry Christmas

NOEL

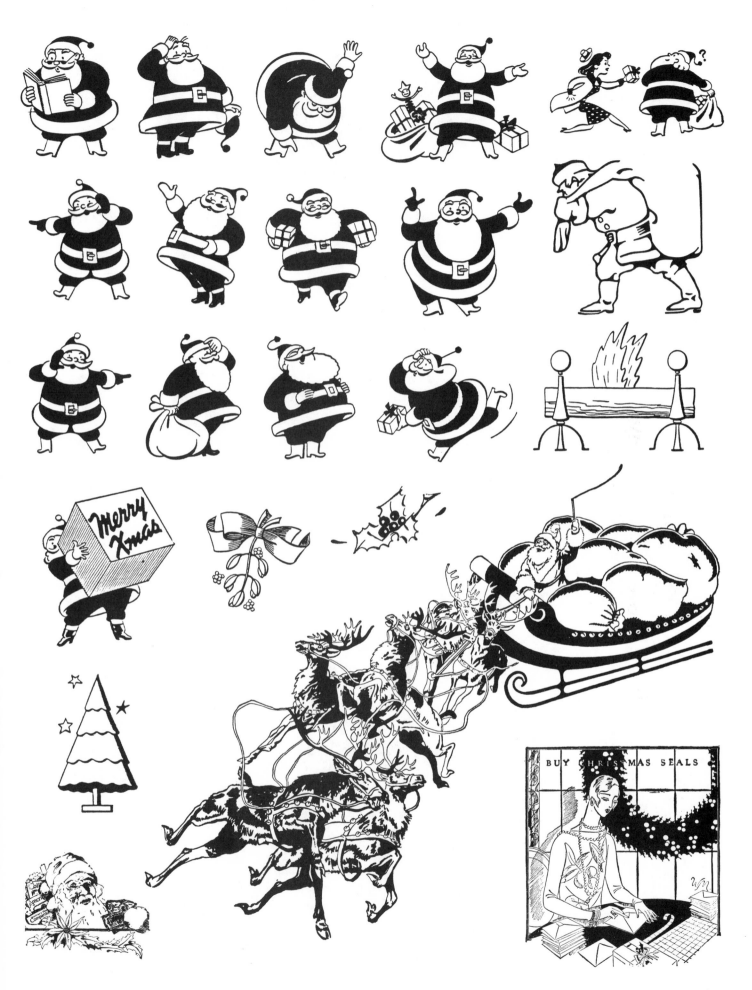

MERRY CHRISTMAS

Merry Christmas!

Yule

CHRISTMAS GREETINGS

MERRY XMAS

CHRISTMAS CHEER

BEAUTY

SALON

BEAUTY SALON

Look your best

HOSE

Beauty Culture

Beauty Shop

Beauty Shop

Beauty Culture

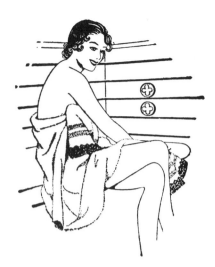

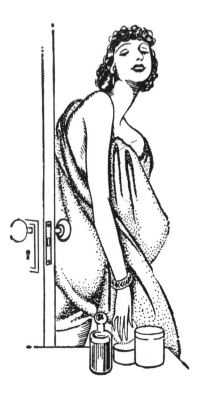

Beauty Shoppe

Beauty Specialists

Manicuring

Beauty Culture

LINGERIE

Gowns

HOSIERY

BEAUTY CULTURE

maison

de beaute

46   Women and Beauty Care

Manicuring

Beauty Salon

Hair Dressers

Permanents   Permanents   Hair Dressers

Beauty Culture   Beauty Culture   Manicuring   Jewelry   Beauty Shop   Permanents   Hair Dressers

Jewelry

Millinery

Hair Dressers

Manicuring

Hair Bobbing

Lingerie

Hair Cutting

Hosiery

Jewelry

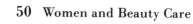  

50   Women and Beauty Care

WHEN I WAS YOUR AGE

PLAYS AND PLAYERS

DANCING

DINE and DANCE

DANCEMUSIC

DANCING

WINES
DOMESTIC / FOREIGN

COCKTAILS

Excellent Food

PLEASANT ATMOSPHERE
Modern MUSIC

Cocktail Lounge

Oh Boy!
WHAT A FLOOR SHOW

Fine Food

COCKTAIL LOUNGE
and RESTAURANT

DINE and DANCE

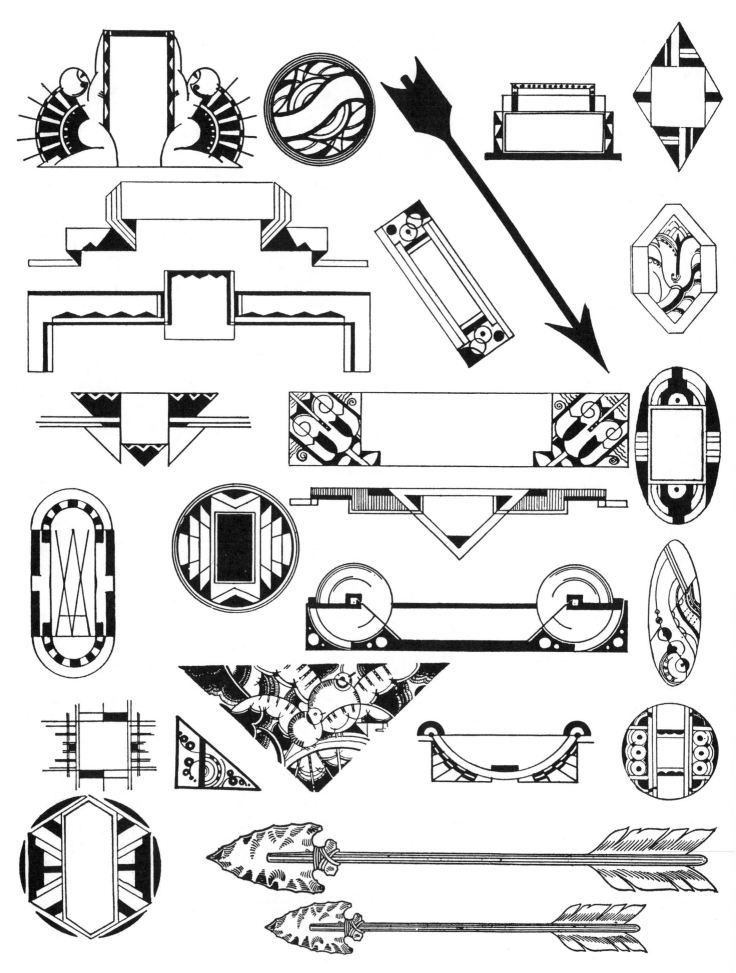

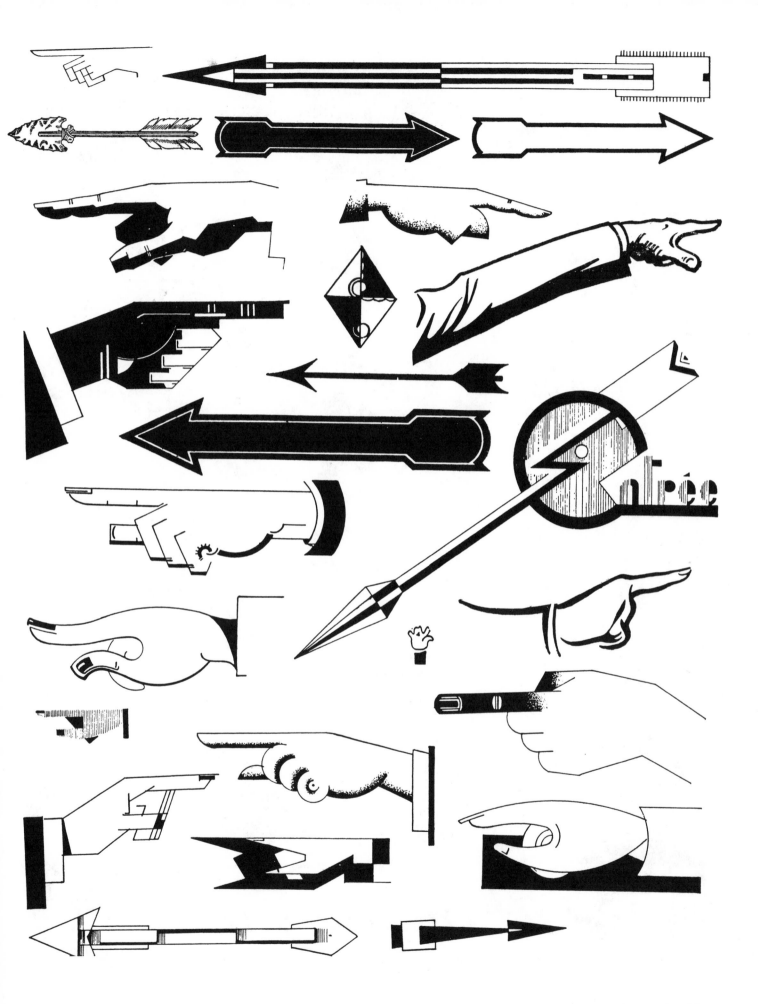

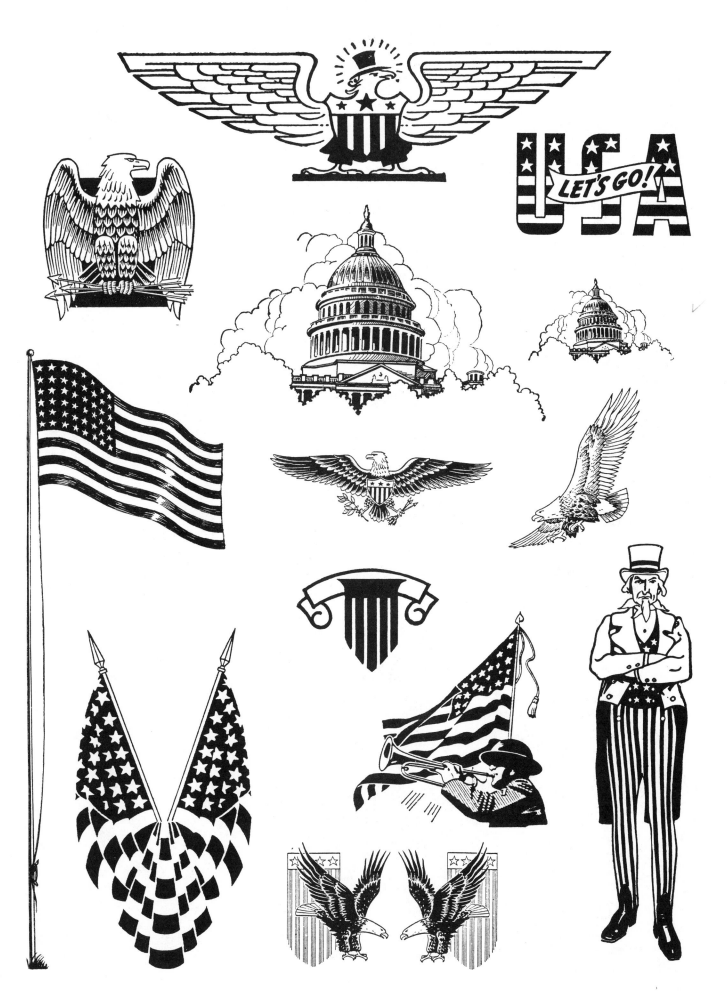